ABSENCE ◆ PRESENCE

ABSENCE ◆ PRESENCE

poems

Christien Gholson

SHANTI ARTS PUBLISHING
BRUNSWICK, MAINE

ABSENCE ◆ PRESENCE

Published by Shanti Arts Publishing
Designed by Shanti Arts Designs

Cover image by Clark Walding, *evanescent*, 2019–2022. Oil, alkyd, and
wax on canvas. 34 x 30.75 inches. Used with the artist's permission.
www.clarkwalding.com | www.charlottjackson.com

Shanti Arts LLC
193 Hillside Road
Brunswick, Maine 04011
shantiarts.com

Printed in the United States of America

ISBN: 978-1-956056-69-3 (softcover)

Library of Congress Control Number: 2022951747

For the empty cobalt sky, and the piñon branches and raven cries that appeared out of that emptiness, on a trail in the foothills of the Santa Fe mountains. Presence born from absence . . .

Contents

Winter ♦ Realm of the Dead

Lunar New Year

Acknowledgments

Grateful acknowledgment is made to the editors of the following journals and presses where these poems previously appeared:

The American Journal of Poetry: "No One's at the Cash Register"; "Ruins: A Poem-Essay"; and "Seven Songs Sung at Reservoir No. 4"

Bitter Oleander: "Balance, A Definition"; "Echoes"; "History"; "Moonrise, February"; "The Sea Approaches: Fever Vision"

Cholla Needles: "Looking South from a Cliff Edge at Cieneguilla Petroglyph Site"; "Shadows, Wandering"; and "Summer Solstice"

Duck Lake Journal: "Stone-Hidden, Whereabouts Unknown"

Hanging Loose Magazine: "After the First Snow"; "Axis Mundi"; and "Vernal Equinox"

Leaping Clear: "No One"; "No One Gets A Box in the Mail"; "No One Listens to the Rain"; "No One Remembers the Beauty of the House Fire"; "No One Watches the Men Talk Behind Podiums"; "This Shape"; "Where Joy Comes From, Where It Goes"; and "Watching a Geminid Meteor Shower with Li Bai"

Serving House Journal: "Dead of Night" and "Drought"

Sky Island Journal: "Delight in the Dark: Prolegomena to a Ceremony for the Dead" and "Facing Night"

All "No One" poems were previously published as a chapbook, *The No One Poems*, by Thirty West Publishing.

Spring ✦ Spells

Vernal Equinox

1

Wind tunnels through sandstone,
coats a trailer with orange dust.
Inside, hands move in sleep, weave
a curse, a blessing.

The dog at the end of the bed
hears something, lifts his head:

mesa shadow
cloud shadow
word shadow

2

The wind extracts a confession
from holes in stone.

Bare canyon trees roar, cut
their teeth on incoherent words.

I forget things:

When was the last surge? Did
I leave the car unlocked? What
do the names El Mozote, Tokhar
and Sangin mean? Why am I
standing here in the dark, holding
a pen?

3

Wind across my face,
plays the holes in my skull
like a flute,

the way a hawk plays
with its own shadow
before it dives . . .

Drought

1

No rain this last fall. No
snow this past winter. The call
of a raven is a splinter
pulled from an old board.

2

I used to love how loneliness
rose from twilit ditch-snow,
how the blue (ombre-blue, ghost's-
embrace-blue) absorbed
the sky, the serpent beneath.
Something was missing, but
something was given.

3

I saw a line of cars—hundreds
of miles, back to back—
heading east, a traveling carnival,
a desperate party, dazzling funeral:
water refugees crossing
the Missouri, the Mississippi.
No one would let them stop
and they drove and drove
through the night, into the sea . . .

4

No rain this last fall. No
snow this past winter. Charcoal
burns. Children on bikes.
Everyone's out enjoying the sun,
the gorgeous sun, the endless
sun, the miracle sun . . .
A horned lizard squeezes out
another live birth.

No One's at the Cash Register

after Han Shan

1

If you're looking for a
peaceful place, this is not it.
I work this register night
after night. "Clean up on
aisle six." Olive oil and glass
and some blood. Red drops.
Chrysanthemum petals. A
woman holds her finger
in a wad of paper towels.
"Did you find everything okay?"
Words here mean nothing. No
use for words on Cold Mountain.
So, why come down? The moon
asked me to pick up some
bananas for her. And cash. I
needed the cash.

2

Middle of the summer
and the frozen vegetables
are still frozen; ice cream,
too. Tourists want a cold
drink, someone to humiliate.
Buying a cold drink is
some kind of competition?
I think of Cold Mountain
and smile, nod. Yes, sir, yes

ma'am, someday you will die.
Me, too! Every once in a while,
someone asks about Cold
Mountain. I point at the
freezer section: it's there,
over there. Everyone
mistakes my finger for the
freezer. What can I do but
laugh?

3

They say: smile more,
you're scaring the customers.
They say: smile less,
you're scaring the customers.
Illusion in the produce
section, illusion in the chip
aisle, illusion between the
coffee and tea. On Cold
Mountain, I remember white
clouds passing, passing
through. But passing through
what, who? Mysteries. Shoppers
pass by all day: pork chops,
broccoli, popcorn, pills, so much
illusion to feed on. This will
make you pretty, this will
make you strong, this will
make you sleep and dream of
peaceful whales—and love.

Clouds, clouds—what is passing
through who? Mystery
feeds us. Illusion
eats us.

4

A customer complained
about me. Several customers
complained. The complaint
was always vague. "Some-
thing is off with him . . . something is missing." The manager,
a drunk, hid behind shelves all
day, spying on me, to see if he
could spot what was wrong.
How is my customer service
smile? I knew what was wrong
but couldn't say. How explain
that I am Cold Mountain mist
through pine, rising. So
many customers are desperate
to leave their anger, their fear,
their sadness inside me, and
walk out of the store free, free
and clear. But it can't be done.
There was No One there. No One
was there . . .

5

I was used to living in some
remote, shaded mountain place.
Cold, cold water and moss: my

only companions. I walked
into this grocery store twenty
years ago and have been here
ever since. Sometimes I think
I am still on the mountain and
this is a dream. Or, the mountain
is a dream and I have always
worked in this store. After work,
I nod to each streetlight in the
parking lot, to the CCTV camera
above the glass door, to the eerie
fluorescent lights in the bank
across the street. Snow and stars
follow me home. Fleas greet me
when I get home, whisper dark
sayings in my ear. I complain,
but the landlord shrugs it off. He
says: I must have brought them
from Cold Mountain.

6

A rich man who bought expensive
bottles of fizzy water told me he
envied me, my simple work, "being
of service." Oh, the challenge, the
people. I was puzzled. Did he think
we stand at these register's day after
day seeking enlightenment? What
world does he live in? But are we all
really living in different worlds? I
reached across the counter, touched
his nose with the end of a carrot.
The carrot was the bridge between

my world and his. He stopped speaking,
mid-sentence, paid in silence. I never
saw him again. Is he silent still? Did
he find his way to Cold Mountain?
Hard to say. It costs nothing
to get there.

7

The night shift manager on duty
says "if you've got time to lean,
you've got time to clean." He's
nervous when it's not busy; wants
to please the authorities inside him,
wants praise. So I compliment his
haircut, his strength. But it doesn't
count: I am No One. I once told
him about beauty, said: "Outside,
the moon flowers white behind
flying clouds." I said: "Look at
the few snowflakes in the streetlight,
against the window glass." I said:
"Nothing lasts." But the words
passed through the hole in the
middle of his body—the wound,
the void—like wind. Voices on
the wind.

8

Professionals like to pretend
they are my friend, sympathize
with my plight. They see an
old man with white hair standing

on his feet all day. O the crushing
boredom. O the years passing in
vain. In vain? Who decides
what's in vain and what's not? If
I was not here, day after day, if I
made my escape back to Cold
Mountain, who would stock the
shelves, who would clean the toilet,
who would be the crazy on the
corner, entertaining you by chanting
the varied history of the labors
of the immortals? O great deciders!
O great patronizing men and women
with your concerned smiles, smiles
that are supposed to warm the hearts
of those who labor, smiles that
allow us to go on with our small,
tired lives. O you who create
the world and destroy the world with
your smile. After work I sometimes
sit beneath a tree, let the wind-across
-leaves wash through me. No smiles.
No frowns. No patronization. No
respect. No one.

9

I have been here at this register
for one hundred years. I could be
here for another hundred more. The
same men will pass through the line,
forever. "Well, looks like everything
will kill you, so I might as well enjoy
myself." Or: "I believe only in what

I can see, taste, smell . . . " Or: "I believe
in almighty God. His power is my
power." Or: "There is a right way
and a wrong way; there are good
guys and bad guys." Or: "I know
what this country needs . . . " I. I. I.
There are refugees, children, in
cages on the border, drinking desert
dust, alone, flying toward their
mothers and fathers in dreams,
never able to reach them, never
able to reach . . . I. I. I. This civilization
is already red dust, in ruins, roof
tiles heaped like fallen leaves. I
could live another hundred years
and still know fear. You see?
No One knows fear.

10

I came down from the mountain.
I work this cash register; I stock
these shelves. I live on the mountain.
I wander among gnarled roots, trace
my finger in patterns of twisted bark.
But Old White-Hair, what are you
saying? How can you be in two places
at once? I'm speaking in tongues again.
So, call me Old-White-Hair-Paradox-
Man. I'm cold and broke, always broke.
My home's a hole and a hole contains
nothing! Not even the wind. Not even
a faint voice on the wind. Emptiness!
No One is drifting home.

Shadows, Wandering

after Li Bai

1

News of a death. Two months gone.

The full moon polishes leftover snow on a distant cliff.

I did not know her well—and what does that mean?

My shadow moves through the shadow of a dead sunflower.

2

The moon circles through bare branches.

I see her face. What were the last words we said to each other?

Everything, absolutely everything tonight, is porous.

My fingers touch the cold, the reflected light, other shadows.

3

A small light flickers on the black mountainside, disappears.

Who could be up there? Dry stalks rub together:

The sound of shadows wandering, looking for the Ancient Way.

I move among stones, then lift my hand, examine it for no reason.

Love in a Time of Chaos

1

Dust reaches the height
of every peak: brown haze,
shifting silhouettes. Some
kind of dark magic; danger,
confusion; and ecstasy
(that eerie light inside a
wall of dust that reveals
the wall to us, to itself).

Blossoms and bees and ashes
whirl . . .

2

A chair sails across stone.
Moans from the mouth
of an empty bucket. New
creatures rise out
of the dark, sink back,
and you touch my hand.
We hold each other
to the bed.

Moths and cigarette butts and
bird bones whirl . . .

3

History is the tantalizing
scent of rain. Promise
of rain (not the actuality)
liberates everything.
The angry dead rise
to the surface to drink,
again. We are the gasp
of water as it hits stone.

Cicadas and war medals and
crushed beer cans whirl . . .

4

A black ant carries a
transparent angel's wing
(so small . . . angel's wings
are so small these days),
and we tell each other
our dreams: words like
caves. Cool relief. Relief
and terror.

Cat's eyes and drones and
nail parings whirl . . .

5

We are earth, un-
earthed; sky, un-skied;
lies, un-lied; with salt
on the skin, without salt;
with water on the tongue,
without water; with
bodies turning in the surf;
with turning away,

without turning away,
we whirl . . .

Delight in the Dark: Prolegomena to a Ceremony for the Dead

1

Today, your death day,
I stood between pear trees,

listened to white blossoms,
bees. Tonight, a hot wind

scrapes the screen: white
petals shoot by, rattle

against the wall like teeth.
The bees sleep: one eye,

one wing, one antenna,
one mind, conjuring

tomorrow's path between
petal, sun, and the dead

who endlessly weave
shadows across stone

and grass. Shifting
patterns across sand.

Everything is alive, alive!
Both dream and reality.

2

We crossed a continent
of lone porch lights

to sit at your table, talk
to you and Jack deep

into the night: Bosch,
nuclear waste trucked

to Yucca mountain,
stagnating wages, Chagall,

union organization, rage
at the wars. A safe base

in the dark, the only place
I ever called home.

Sold now. Maybe razed.
October moths

at the screen, frantic
to merge with porch light,

shining on the last cricket's
song in dry grass.

3

"I'm talking to the dead
again," I say. You say:

"How can I be dead?
We're talking." We talk

in your dimly lit office,
a converted porch.

Tax files on the shelf
behind you, reflections

in dark glass. "Am I
really dead?" you say.

I say: "No, no, you
can't be . . . because I'm

talking to you." A
child's logic. You can't

be: because blossoms,
because bees, because

crows bank against
the wind.

4

A red-brown spider
creates the pattern

of a lemniscate on
the bedroom wall,

symbol of the infinite,
framing the void

inside it all ... I called
you from a phone booth

in Omaha, told you
I'd run out of cash,

might not have enough
gas to make it.

Hearing your voice—
a mix of mirth

and concern—got me
there. A small,

weird miracle inside
this small, weird life:

140 miles on empty,
under a vast night sky.

5

We are smoking outside
a community theater

production of King Lear.
My first Shakespeare!

Your laugh on the empty
street: "That was terrible,

wasn't it?" Is this what
it's like to be an adult?

Because you thought I
knew good Shakespeare

from bad. It was terrible.
The actor leapt around,

desperate to embody
the words. Shouts

in place of meaning,
while someone shook tin

in the wings. *Sturm und
drang.* All the different

worlds inside us never
really leave us, do they?

Seventeen, forty-eight,
sixty-four, eighty-one,

it all spirals around us,
frail, ephemeral, looking

for a way out. Or in. I
hear your teen voice, 1941:

"That was terrible, wasn't it?"
Delight in the dark.

6

Blossoms in moonlight
mimic snow. The first

spring cricket sings
beyond a stone wall.

What is home? I once
looked into your kitchen

window from outside,
at midnight, saw the reflection

of someone long dead,
nameless. "Who are you?"

A useless question, but
I knew—some ancestor,

unknown. Through you,
your house, all the people

who came and went,
there was the possibility

of connection—to a history,
to a lineage; and so,

to the earth, and so to the
silence of frost on grass

(frail, ephemeral, cold as
iron); and so, to the silence

that floats in and out of
all our stories, unnoticed;

and so, to the silence that
holds us so close at the end.

7

Jack once played me *Le Mystere
des Voix Bulgares*, a lamenting

women's choir, dissonant, diachronic; half-western, half-eastern,

and I said: "It sounds like sorrow.
Or joy. I can't tell which." Around

the corner, you sat in your office,
working, deep into the night,

and I eventually drifted in,
to talk, going on about choices

(young enough to believe I had
more control than is possible

in this life). You looked out
the window at the bare box-elders,

snow beyond, and said: "We didn't
have as many choices as you have

now . . . I think that might have
been a good thing." What is fate?

A red-brown spider creating
a lazy-eight on the wall? What is

fate? A story no one can fully
know until we're dead.

8

It snowed on the blossoms
yesterday. Maybe no pears

this year. Blossoms and
pollen and bees spiral

through me: you hand me
cigarettes to deliver

to an old woman abandoned,
alone, in an old folk's home.

There's a story, there's
always a story: her daughter

rescued her from death
decades before. (You imply

it was an act of revenge
for a terrible childhood.)

The old woman had wanted
a swift death, but then

outlived everyone she knew.
Except you. I spend

the afternoon with her,
talking, smoking. All around:

twisted hands, wheel-chairs
parked in the void, caught

between heaven and a
urine stench. Why did you

send me here? Because
cottonwood seed is on

the wing? Because the old
woman and I have both

become ghosts to ourselves,
need the touch of another

ghost to be able to touch
the earth again? Or was it

just another chore that
you couldn't do today?

Either way, we talk and
smoke and smoke and

talk in the shade. Blossoms
and pollen and bees

spiral through us. A crow
banks against the wind.

9

Your last role:
Eleanor of Aquitaine

in *The Lion in Winter.*
Eleanor, Eleanor,

condemned to her
own castle, but still

wily, acerbic. Her
words the pin

that continually
picked all the king's

locks: "In a world
where carpenters

get resurrected,
anything is possible."

You were not
Eleanor. But you

could play Eleanor.
Darkness in delight.

10

I see your house now the way
I saw Jack's painting of a circus

tent on a flat plain. What was
behind that flap? A chorus of

diachronic moths, lamenting joy?
Figures with Day-Glo wigs,

posing in the dark? The papier-
mâché detritus from a production

of Ionesco's *Rhinoceros*? A lone
clown playing Satie on a lone

piano, lit by the moon? Or the
dawn wind, carrying the scent

of all the grass it's passed through—
Rockies to plains to prairie—

right past your porch. You step
out of your house, into a

box elder tree, wrap yourself
in a cloak of bark . . .

11

What is praise? The way
the thrasher's yellow eye,

earlier today, studied
something between two

stacked stones. What is
love? The way pear blossoms,

right now, light the dark
closest to the tree.

What is beauty? The shape
of the space you left behind

when you died—the space
between stars, the infinite

space between two stones.
Tonight, I'll go outside,

whisper your name into
the dark. I expect to find

silence, the silence that
holds us so close at the end.

I also expect that I'll hear
you whisper back.

What will you say?

i.m. Marita Mastrofski (1924–2016)

Summer ◆ Fire

Summer Solstice

1

Arugula, gone to seed. Fire-
white petals at the end of each
stalk. Fire in the mountains.

Deep inside burning summer
stones it's cool, cool as the touch
of Mary-from-Below. Noon,

noon, and everything is trying
to find that cool, cool place
deep inside . . .

2

Fireball on the highway, can't
get to the airport. Traffic backed
up southbound. Smear of black,

a shadow across macadam, across
the barrier wall. Glass glitters and
someone's car stalls. Inside

the shadow: everything that could
have been. Passing, I have the
sudden desire to begin again . . .

3

The old man with his embryo sign
at *Southwest Women's Options*
is shy. Won't speak to me. He stands

in the full heat, shoulders hunched,
body in retreat, stares down a car.
Distant fire-ball and smoke: does he

believe that the heart is an embryo,
desperate to burn, desperate to be
cooled by Mary-from-Below?

4

The storyteller sits beneath
the bedroom window of the
woman widowed by the crash.

He's made of sandsmoke; rose
from a dry riverbed when
the explosion shook the earth

around him. He lives off grief,
the heat radiating from the street.
He listens to her breathe.

5

Mary-from-Below scrawls her sign
on an abandoned freight car's side.
The young widow lifts her hand

in the middle of the night to ward
something off. Sirens, sirens, and
the dream of fire inside a humming-

bird's heart. She wakes alone, knows
she is pregnant, that someone is
listening to her breathe.

6

There was rain. The last desperate
attempt of the spider curled in dust
to bring down the sky. Chollas

bounced back, after wandering
the borderland between here and death.
Pear leaves brush each other, sound

like water, like distant waves—the way
flies on a carcass sound like
distant human speech.

7

We are apart. 1200 miles:
the space between the hummingbird and the stone. We keep

missing each other on the phone.
The Storyteller roams around here
at night; stopping, staring, searching

for Mary-from-Below. He holds
out his heart, a stone he found in a
busy Dollar Store parking lot.

No One Remembers the Beauty
of the House Fire

Flames leapt
beyond their own
smoke, toward rings
of cold light
around a full moon.
No One stood vigil,
witness to the lust
shining off the eyes
of the bystanders,
the relief of flame-
shadows across
so many faces. No One
knew they were
all cradling the same
word inside them
(with love, with repulsion):

Beautiful . . . Beautiful . . .

No One rushed up
the front steps, grabbed
the car keys inside
the front door. A vortex
of flame raged at
No One's face (staring
into the open mouth
of some hideous god,
lost, bellowing its
first and last word,

the word that brought
death-by-fire
into being . . .). Just as
it reached No One, it
turned up towards
the second floor, following
some other prey,

a stream of heretical words,
erotic, repulsive:

Beautiful . . . Beautiful . . .

Seven Songs Sung at Reservoir No. 4

after Du Fu

1

A wanderer on this path—thousands of miles
from home. Look across the water: the world

on the surface is what is left of the world. On TV,
the endless replay of another shooting. Small fish

move through the dark beneath, carry the dead
on their backs. One dead, two dead, a dragonfly's

wing-song leads me to my first song sung here,
on the lost art of knowing which stones can speak

the names of the dead, the lost art of knowing what
"home" means, the lost art of gravity . . .

2

Do the dead wonder why they are riding the backs
of such small fish? Three dead, four dead. They

ask why they didn't land on the back of an
ocean flatfish, eyes forced towards the bottom,

scanning for salvation among phosphorescent
angels with huge, ravenous mouths. O song,

my second song sung for the grief to come,
sinking slowly through layers of red cold, blue

cold, blind cold, through the freezing bones of
this generation, through the next, the next . . .

3

Slight ripples cut the pines into cubes, needles
bob in place: a fly's breath, a faint word spoken

from below? Five dead, six dead, no point of
origin; waves born before *before*. It's always

the same deadened faces, for the last one hundred
years, the last two hundred—wearing mourning-

masks, pious, excreting feeble thoughts and
prayers. Someone's making money somewhere.

Fuck your Prayers is my third song sung, to
drown-out the dead who feed on the dead . . .

4

Have you seen them? It's so hard to see them
through the sun's reflection. You have to wait,

and wait, then: seven dead, eight dead, nine dead.
Clouds pass through the water. The dead now

ride the fish in the sky. Medieval images, a
haunted call for the end, apocryphal; and soft,

so soft, can you hear it? Ten dead. Eleven.
I play useless witness again and again, in this,

my fourth song, boots sunk in cold mud, this
my shadow song, sung to my own reflection . . .

5

I am so far from almost everyone I know,
the desert I love. Twelve dead, thirteen. Do

they see the same sun, moon, as me? Everyone
lives in a different world now, a world of

personal design: customized. Messages float
across the surface, through ripples of distant

trees, fall asleep enfolded in cold depths, slip
through dark branches. I re-assemble them as

my fifth song: of an oak leaf caught in a vine
last fall, hung above cold ground . . .

6

What am I looking for? The joke of wisdom?
My own heart? A stone that knows my name?

Fourteen dead, fifteen dead. Fish-mouths kiss
the surface of the water. Something must be

sacrificed. For freedom. For money. For the
money that is freedom. So, duck. Duck and

cover. Gunfire in the distance. Deer hunters.
Sixteen dead. Seventeen. I wait for the second

blast, this my sixth song, the song that must
appear in the space between shots . . .

7

Everything is happening at once. Thirty-six
dead, forty-seven. Keep counting, don't stop

counting. A bubble rises to the surface. Sixty-
five dead, seventy-eight. Another bubble rises,

floats in the sun. Everything is happening at once.
Always has. I mimic the sound of the bubble

as it reaches the surface, the sound of the sun
burning across the bubble's thin sheen, the sound

of the emptiness inside stretched to its limit,
this, my seventh and last song sung . . .

Dragon in the Rock

Shadow in the cupola at the top of the long horse-snout
where the left eye watches me; curious, fierce.

Every rock has a name the dead must learn to sing

Green crustose lichen tattooed across his side, where
feathers, flaps, and flags of desire once clung, now solidified.

Every rock was once a flame

Circle of orange-yellow lichen, mid-forehead. Third eye
follows the progress of four ravens in the valley below.

Every rock is a mouth keeping the silence before the name

Black wings, black bodies merge, separate. A continually changing
black hieroglyph: grass-sorrow, pinyon-laughter, heart-lightning...

Every rock is continually unraveling back to the place it was made

Wind through juniper, he rides flying snow-dust, escapes
this geo-spell for a few seconds, body equal to the sun.

The dead sing the names, but they don't know yours,
they don't know yours, will never know yours

The Sea Approaches: Fever Vision

Dust flies through the valley, scrapes the Jemez peaks.
Dark silhouettes break through the dust, jagged under stars,
the fish inside their eyes scour a shallow Inland Sea, spiral
around hungry weeds anchored to rock, ephemeral
as threads of ink in water; languid, spreading.

The sea approaches.

I am a word made of blood-muscle, white matter,
gray matter, salted bone, star-aureoles, following
the fish, its silent trail of hunger, making a map
of how desire shapes the body. We are both flying
toward the sea at incredible speed.

The sea approaches.

The mountains begin their slow walk across
the moon's surface, towards my door, my bed;
their inexhaustible black eyes dissolve my body, re-shape me
from scattered belemnite tentacle fossils, into a proto-
squid wreathed in darkness.

The sea approaches.

Sea levels rise, swamp concrete steps, swamp cemeteries.
Coffins rise. What was once hidden has become visible.
This sea inside—spun from agony-masks, a ritual murder,
when hunger was love—mirrors the Holy Sea, that blind
blue phantom face, that first face . . .

The sea approaches.

No One Watches the Men Talk Behind Podiums

No One watches the press conference
over and over. Words endlessly

tumble out of official mouths. Insects
sucked dry. No One wonders how

these men managed to open holes
in the world with such shriveled words.

Holes that let the dead back in. All
the dead who believe they are owed

a second, a third, a fourth chance.
Endless repetitions: *I'll get it right*

this time. Victory will be my sun-
chalice, a golden wall. No One runs

outside, watches the hummingbird
moths in the lavender. Their wing-

chants, counterpoint to the sound
of bees. Tongues arc toward purple

blossoms. For a few seconds,
the tongues fill the holes torn in

the earth, the sky, in so many hands,
faces, torsos. When the moths speed

off, the holes return. No One breathes
in the trance-inducing lavender scent,

feels the dead words stir the air . . .
the dead words stir and stir . . .

Echoes

1

This canyon tricks the ear by its
tricks of space: stone ridges, corridors,
echoes inside a labyrinth of stone cul-de-sacs.
Somewhere, a trumpet plays *Summertime*.
Summertime rises from a hidden blue room
or falls from a falling orange sky. No way
to find the point of origin . . .

2

Years ago, I listened to a ghost
play sax between the back of an abandoned
gas station and a rail line embankment.
Never seen, never seen, held together by
half-memorized Coltrane solos. Music
that pulled loneliness from my body, showed
it to my face, like the still-beating heart
to a grateful sacrifice.

3

Coyotes sing over a kill a half-mile off.
Their voices mingle with the trumpet, sound
as if they are just beyond the fence. Once,
at midnight, while I let stars crawl in and out
of my coat, my coat, I heard a woman
whisper to someone: *I'm sorry, I love you, but* . . .
It could have come from anywhere on earth.

4

Summertime ends. I shout into the night.
No words, just a voice full of joy, of joy,
trying to reach itself across time and space.
When it returns, it sounds like a raven's head
laughing at the bottom of an empty well.

Autumn • All the Worlds

Autumnal Equinox

1

Dead lizard inside a window-hinge well. Brittle,
nothing but a skin-shell. Must have been folded-in,
crushed last fall. How long before death was welcome?
I hold the paper-light body in my palm. Individual
scales drift off. Gray snow, death seeds. They mate
with mint leaves. Next year, haidomyrmex ants will
emerge from the earth.

2

Gray skies. The last pear sways in the wind.
I think of so many children's school photos: that
eager smile, those sad eyes. *Can you love me?*
Can I be loved?

3

The old feeling that everything is illusion has
returned. Mars burns above Picacho, taunts me.
Spears, helmets, a trigger finger; children's shoes,
empty. No way to find the touch that's real. Shadows
at the corner of the eye. A bird or spirit or ghost-hive
plunges through the dark.

4

Yesterday, while doing laundry, a cottonwood
across the canyon turned yellow. It happened
between ten and noon. Later, we stood together,

staring, taking it in, stunned innocent as lizards—
what is this world?

5

War and work, always there, always waiting.
Someone stole my credit card info, was flagged
across town. They were desperate, I was desperate.
A moon crests the ridge, one of a thousand that will
rise tonight. Lit from behind, the mountain's head
and shoulders are still, waiting, poised to strike.

6

Everything has become a cave painting, exposed
in the light, exposed by the cool wind. Our eyes
whirl in dark sockets. Hummingbirds battle among
pear leaves. They drink from my body, from yours,
and during the night, they dip long beaks into the space
where lizard scales have fallen away.

7

I sit on the stone wall, look down into the canyon:
streetlights, lights of houses. I keep slipping in and out
of so many worlds. Past, future. Indigo worlds, parchment
worlds, worlds without name. At the base of the pear tree,
stringy cowpen daisies glow with their own light.

Where Joy Comes From, Where It Goes

after Wang Wei

Alone I come back to this piñon, how it clings
to a seam of stone, precarious. Resin

on the fingers: turpentine, with a hint of orange.
What water tastes like to the dead?

A chickadee pulls a seed from a cone. Look away,
look back, she's no longer there. All my thoughts—

how I can't, how I can, how it's too late – dissolve.
Wind moves the sun across piñon branches.

Spirals of light: how they hold the mind together,
how they take it apart . . .

Dead of Night

after Du Fu

Window glass trembles against wood. A hum
inside the skull wakes me from a dream: a child
hiding in the well of a car as it rolls backwards
down a mountain road. No driver, no brakes.

I step outside, barefoot, night-sweat freezing
against the skin, look up into the engine noise,
believe for a second the stars have finally broken
free of all law, spinning around each other.

Planes, so many planes, all heading west—
Utah, Nevada? Red lights, green lights, white;
lights to keep each other in line, keep each other
close. Training maneuvers.

Afterwards, silence rises from the earth, nearby
stones; a silence deeper than before the planes,
before the dream. Eisenhower, Pershing, Grant
and Washington settle back into red dust.

What is this thing called *human progress*? Why
do we believe in it? Left-over snow gleams
against rock on Picacho's north side. A dog
barks in the canyon below.

Axis Mundi

1

What's found in the heart? A stack
of old magazines; a small box

cradling one tack; a book of matches;
a flying ant, lying on the pavement,

exhausted. Your heart was too weak
to handle what the surgeons did.

Were you exhausted, too? Too
exhausted to hang on.

2

Inside a darkroom, images appear
slowly: a sharp concrete corner,

blue sky beyond; symmetry of posts,
dunes . . . textures, colors, forms . . .

sometimes a face. I see you shoot
and re-shoot, as if the lens would

show something more, something
the eye, or words, could never reveal.

To find the world beneath the world?
Or to put the world (and so the mind)

back together?

3

You once took a series of photos of me,
staged, crouching with a dead butterfly

in my hands. Blue wings, lattice of black.
I felt I'd finally made it into a monograph

by Diane Arbus (You introduced me
to Arbus: photos of the forgotten half-

seconds before or after the shock of love,
terror, or loneliness passes through us . . .)

Halfway through the shoot I realized
the insect was not dead, was still dying.

When it died, something slipped through
the skin, into my blood, found its way

to the back of my skull. I was exhilarated,
violated, horrified . . . the blue-black seed

of future poetry.

4

Lo Mein or burgers. Always Lo Mein
or burgers. We ate in your grandparent's

living room, behind the restaurant kitchen,
in front of their huge TV, a metal fan

rattled behind us. Outside, to the east,
behind the restaurant, one hundred

thousand insects no one will ever name,
built the night out of their cries.

To the south, the white-glare and din
of the dog-track. To the north, a motel.

Out front, to the west, Highway 17:
cars heading to Miami, Silver Springs

and the glass bottom boats; and we
sat at the center, *Axis Mundi*, bare feet

on cool shag, a rare calm inside me,
as chaos revolved around us. Riot fires,

war, and assassins far, far away, beyond
your family's restaurant—a refuge, *the*

refuge, the center; open, empty . . .

5

We stood in the shade of an archway, on
the Champs-Elysees, waiting for our sisters

to finish window-shopping. You gave me
a running commentary on everyone who

passed, saying things I was not allowed
to say, things I was not allowed to think.

Joyful, snarky, appalling. Sometimes I
thought of us as brothers. *Brothers?* Such

a strange word to us both. I once told you
I remembered we cut our thumbs, mingled

our blood. You shook your head. *We never
did that.* You were right. I made it up. I was

always making things up. I still do.

6

I'm held together by all the lizard's eyes
in the yard, by the vicious beauty of the sun

(fierce, peeling everything from itself). Where
are you now? I see stacks of newspapers,

magazines, files—who knows what they
will find in your room? Were you lonely?

There were times—decades ago—I was so
lonely I couldn't answer your lonely letters,

asking questions no one could ever answer.
Questions I refused to ask myself.

7

The heart is a house on fire, under
a full moon—terrifying, achingly

beautiful. Did everyone get out in time?
There were so many stairs. I ascended

and descended those stairs, looking
for you. When we finally met, on a

remote, wooden landing, walls burning
around us, we held each other . . .

for a second, two seconds . . . and then
you were gone.

i.m. Gary Loo 1960–2018

No One Listens to the Rain

1

Darkness builds.
Rain batters stone.
Thunder to the east
and No One hears
the soft, terrible words
uttered by the first
to stumble onto
the massacre-site.

2

Wind blows open
the door. The world
below follows
the scent of water
up to the surface.
No One hears
ancestors break
through dead leaves,
lift patches of dirt,
part small stones.

3

Mist-rise off
the south ridge;
vapor turns in
on itself. No One
marks the space

between drops, hears
the child curled
inside the second
before her father's
last breath.

4

The bent bough
absorbs rain, shakes
off rain. No One
hears fire, pages
softly curling black,
small flames trans-
forming words
to holes. Holes
merge.

5

No One stares
into the black eye
of a fence lizard.
It blinks and the
world disappears.
When the world
reappears the rain
has stopped.

6

Hollyhock buds
open. Yellow
mouths and red

mouths swallow
hummingbird
moth's whole.
No One hears
their wings
beat against
the wall of the
plant's gullet;
psychopomps,
leading the rain
down . . .

Looking South from a Cliff Edge at La Cieneguilla Petroglyph Site

Wind kicks up dust all day.

Dead grass rattles. Dust
refracts dusk-light: gray-
pink, gray-blue, gray-purple,
gray-green. Sangres to the
east, shadows of angled buttes
to the west (layers of rock
playing hide and seek with
the earth).

Vast flats, to the border.

Bodies out there, dis-
appeared. Unfound, un-
buried. Piñon rakes
the wind. There's so much
space here I open my arms,
inside this world of
prisons and empty
plastic bottles.

A sudden flash of light:

maybe an old woman,
unable to pay her electricity
bill, lifting a flashlight
to the photo of her dead son;

or the last of the sun
reflected off an old Spanish
helmet, surfacing, trying to
find its way home . . .

Balance, A Definition

What I Found:

In a dry wash at twilight, on cold sand,
a cairn, three feet high, intricately balanced.

Close to the cairn's foundation, a deer's
hoof-print, sunk deep. Just one, no others.

A Few Questions:

Why did those awkward and precarious angles of stone
            re-open an old dream of floating (floating trees,
half-moon and stars below roots; floating stones,
            imitating hawks . . .)?

How did a deer pass so close to the cairn
                        without knocking it down?

Who first said *float* but really meant *sink*?

Some Answers:

The deer appeared from the space between the stones.

The cairn appeared when the deer floated by
                        and touched down one hoof, testing reality.

And the sky, the sky, with its thousand
            interlocking blue staircases, built from nothing
        but air and the breath of the dead, appeared
            out of the dark atrial chamber of the deer's heart . . .

Ruins: A Poem-Essay

Introduction: Abandoned Farmhouse, Southern Iowa

An upturned piano
in the front room.
Last chords struck
decades ago, still
in the air. Sound
folded inside no-
sound. A spiral
of ceiling plaster
on the floorboards.
Outside: a rose bush
and one rose.
A figure bends
to the rose, sings
O rose, thou art sick . . .

Innocence: World War I Trench; Nimy, Belgium

A shell-casing
beneath dirt. I looked
down the long ravine
dotted with old trees,
saw the shape of
the trench, and the angels
of Mons screamed
out of the sky, for
the righteous army,
for the great cause, for
Venus and Mars.
It all happened
long ago, so long ago,

when people died
in useless wars, when
angels dodged bullets,
when the world was mud
and horror . . . so long ago,
not like today . . . Here:
the sun, then rain, then
leaves. We won't ever
have to fight. And we
will never die.

Romance: Tintern Abbey; Monmouthshire, Wales

Orange and red larches
on the hill. Smoke, low
in the valley. Cold, cold
stone and a crow flew
beneath a skeleton arch
(once stained-glass), landed
on cold grass and laughed.
A tour guide, in Cistercian
robes, told us how
the eighteenth century rich
haunted the abbey at night,
waited for ghosts. I saw
torches chasing shadows
across stone; suddenly
heard how the occasional
shout from the quarry
and lime kiln nearby
broke the aesthetic spell.
Noises from an underground
realm. Demons, trolls . . .
but the old red sandstone

in moonlight was beauty
itself, wasn't it? The crow
lifted off the grass and I
waited for the underworld
creatures that have hunted
the rich ever since
to come out of their holes . . .

Fear of Death: Farm Gravesite;
Grasslands National Monument, Colorado

Earth and sky and
wind through grass.
A wood windmill
grinds out a few words.
This . . . this . . . this
is a nail through a
sun-cracked board . . .
this . . . this . . . this
is a flake of rust
sifted off the nail
in the sun . . . this is
the gravesite of a girl,
ten years old, behind
where the house used
to stand. Sing it: she
drank the incessant
wind, the dark humors,
on the wrong day
and sank. And the
house followed her
into the earth.
In a nearby corral,
a lone pony eyed us, tail

swatting off flies.
Who are you? What
do you know?
As we walked back
to the car, we heard
it gallop and gallop
behind us and could not
look back, knew
the girl was going
for a ride . . .

Prophesy: Pueblo Ruins, Bandelier National Monument

Three spires of stone
guard the empty rooms
cut into stone. Sun-dust,
shade-cliffs, three
spires and a charred tree.
A face emerges from
the burnt bark: a bear,
an old man. It stares
at the kids scrambling up
a kiva ladder, then makes
obeisance to the three spires,
and disappears. A bobcat
turns, slinks deeper into
its own shadow. Something
has happened; nothing
has happened. An
infinitesimally small shift
in time and space?
The great Absence born
from this Presence? The three
have lived this before,

will again. All things
born from their gaze, witness
to the eternal falling
away and return . . .

Acknowledging Transience: Hotel Ruins; Mt. Overlook, New York

What is the attraction?
Space that once held
something. Something
someone put into motion
with words. Put this
here, put that there,
build this with concrete,
that with steel. *We're
going to make so much
money* . . . Those who
spoke the words have
entered the same space.
Space inside space.
I stand inside the
emptiness, look through
the holes in concrete,
and feel relief, sudden relief,
knowing there is only
change, that the wind
never moves around me,
but through the empty space
already inside.

Acceptance of Death: Pennard Castle, Gower, Wales

The castle sits in sand,
edge of a cliff, next
to a golf course. Snails
fill the cracks between
stone, hold the fortress
together. Here
a Norman prince refused
to invite the fairies
to his wedding, so they
cursed the castle
with drifting sand, and it
had to be abandoned.
Invaders, invaded. What
was the last night and day
here like? After the lord
and lady were already
settled in their new castle,
further inland? Did
the night watchman stare
into Three Cliffs Bay,
try to interpret the sayings
of the wind-against-seafoam?
Come morning, did he
go down to the beach
and find great blue heron prints
in wet sand, walking into
the sea? And did he follow
those prints into the water,
marry the heron in a chapel
beneath the waves?
He did.

Closing: The Stars, The Nation, The Stars

after Robinson Jeffers

Midnight: a cricket
stops his rhythm,
waits to see
if my movements
are dangerous or not.
The volunteer Lamb's Ears,
all silver, illuminate
low clouds. Why do
I suddenly remember
how someone used
to blow a Shofar
in this canyon at sunset?
Years ago. A haunted
sound. The hands,
the mouth. Where are they
now? There's a break
in the clouds and I see
a few stars. What the poet
Erling Friis-Baastad
calls *fossil light*: light
thrown into space before
water, before the fish's eye;
before the finger pointing
at the night sky. A night sky
of the already dead,
still shining . . .

Watching a Geminid Meteor Shower
with Li Bai

Asteroids whip flammable gas
into flame—brief streaks of light
between seemingly immortal stars.
A brilliant white line scars the night
beneath Orion's belt, across
Eridanus (river of souls), pierces
the mind, mirrors the flash
across a synapse. Messages sent
from before the earth was formed.

Li Bai dove into the moon . . .

I stand on a stone wall, shivering,
feet cold, watch stone after stone burn
the night sky alive. Anchored to earth,
the mind rides the brief light. Li Bai
stands behind me, drunk, a shade
in the shadow of a pear tree,
his dark eyes on a similar light-shower
fifteen hundred years gone.

Li Bai dove into the moon . . .

Spontaneous noises—whoops and
sighs—erupt from my mouth after
each flash: the nervous system
recognizing itself . . . The afterimage
haunts the eye: an eerie black light.

Here, then not here; same as me, as
Li Bai, last poet to hunt after immortality,
knowing the search was futile, a joke;
knowing a life of poetry can be
made in pursuit of that very joke.

Li Bai dove into the moon . . .

Winter ✦ Realm of the Dead

Winter Solstice

1

The sound
of iron on iron
travels sun
to sun, feeds
off pale light.

Voices ride
the cold.

2

A woman slumps
on the curb, counts
her change, repeats
out loud the incessant
word-pattern in her
head:

conspicuous sedition
sorrowful mechanism
reason for the season
reason for the treason

3

The dead rabbit,
roadside,
waits to step
into its own shadow.

4

He can't remember
his name. His breath
hangs in the air: water.
Water and salt.

A car pulls up, his daughter
gets out. Her breath
hangs in the air: water.
Water and angry thoughts.

Where have you been?

5

Cartilage of a
guitarfish inside
a cloud; cloud
inside a Stellar Jay's
eye; Stellar Jay flies
through a woman
on the curb; a man
hands her a few
pennies . . .

I wake, find a penny
on the windowsill.

6

A penny for your
thoughts. Penny
Dreadful. What is
a penny worth?

Black branches
weave the songs
of the dead
into a red horizon.

Pennies on the eyes.

7

A rusted water tank.
Cold gathers beneath it.
I tap the side:
emptiness taps back.

After the First Snow

1

A perfect sphere
of snow sits atop
the last standing post
of a fallen fence.
The wars go on. And
on. But there's
no more news. A snow-
covered pear branch
looks like a deer
femur. We go
to work, come home,
eat dinner, talk.
Magpie claw-prints
in snow-dust
across gutter ice. I
remark how
the moon and the snow
make the shadows—
of trees, stones, parked
cars, telephone poles—
more real than
the things
themselves.

2

Bright moon, clear
sky, blue snow.
Something moves

beyond the bedroom window.
I turn, want it
to be a face,
a stranger's face, asking
sacrifice for all
the dead—
a finger bone, an eye,
the ecstatic part of me
that lives inside
a cholla thorn,
lit orange
by the setting sun—
but there is
nothing there,
never anything
there.

History

1

Follow the curve of a juniper root,
plunged deep into stone, see how
it tunnels past drunk fathers, brutal mothers
shielding themselves from their own
brutal childhood with a raised bible; groping
grandfathers, great-grandmother's who spent
their final years staring out windows, silent.

2

Bare birch limbs lit white by the low sun
cast thin shadows across the road. A village
on fire, a woman left for dead. She looks
up through the flames at the same moon I see:
moon craters, a moon-rabbit, shadows
of moon-children grasping each other's hands,
playing some dark game, silent.

3

Follow the curve of cholla arms; thin, thin,
silvered with thorns: some point into
the darkening sky, some into the ground,
gestures learned and repeated for centuries—
the way I startle when ravens scream, the way
I stare at the moon, desperate to understand
the game those dark children play, silent.

No One Gets a Box in the Mail

for Freya

1

Wind kicks snow-dust into the sun.
A box arrives on No One's doorstep.
The box is filled with singed letters,
smoke-damaged, thirty years old: ghost
loves, a non-existent father. Ink fades
into the page. Snow dust's crystal prism
breaks the pale winter light, reveals
purple, green, red: light turned inside out.
There is a letter from No One's grand-
mother. No One opens it. She says how
much she liked No One's description
of desert snow. No One puts the paper
down, looks out the window, confused.
No One wrote about desert snow
thirty years ago?

2

In the letters: aftermath of a house fire,
a car crash, break-ups. Someone talks
of love, then talks of love lost. There are
photos with no faces—a butte, a telephone
booth, an ice covered 7-11 parking lot.
No One remembers. Cheyenne. Newspapers to keep warm in a VW bug.
And waking, shivering, shocked. Not
from the fear of freezing to death, but
of disappearing, never truly seen.

3

Long shadows across blue snow. No
One wonders if there is anyone left alive
out there who knows their words are being
read once again? Does the sound come
to them in half-sleep? The sound of ice
wrapping itself around a spider's husk, still
hanging in a web outside the bedroom
window; or maybe the sound of branch-
shadows moving slowly across a
coyote fence?

4

Moonlight tightens its grip on bare
apple branches. No One dreams of an
old woman, scratching the symbol for
snowdust-in-moonlight on an oracle bone:
a pair of wings woven into a rain of dark
stars (signifying light turned inside out).
No One watches her place the symbol
face-down on the cold ground. No One
knows time and death cannot be cheated,
or changed, but there is the hope that

the image will fuse with the earth,

will fuse with the earth,

will fuse . . .

Moon Rise, February

The moon is a hollow bird skull, landscape of holes,
threaded by the wind, rising past a giant white cross.

An old man with trembling hands crosses himself.
See the pile of hands and feet, lit on fire in the plaza?

For Christ, always for Christ. The shadow of a crow
swallows the last of the sun: transubstantiation.

The moon passes through me, leaves behind an ant hill
in a dry river, dead Franciscans still on trial for torture,

for murder. The old man looks down at his open palms.
What does he see? The blood and the body? The holy

trinity of crow prints in snow? Ochre prints on a cave
wall? I look into my own palms:

Stone-Hidden, Whereabouts Unknown

after Chia Tao

"I asked the boy beneath the pines.
He said: the master's gone alone,
herb picking somewhere on the mount,
cloud-hidden, whereabouts unknown."

I was not looking for him. But there he was:
a series of fin-like stones—a spine slowly sinking,
or struggling to emerge—out of the mountain.

A nearby cairn, made of thin shale, his apprentice,
said his master was deep inside the earth, gathering
words. Words? What kind of words?

(This is a poem about how dragons slip
in and out of my body, fly beneath the surface)

He is gathering the words that pass between
the mouth of a dead piñon root and the mandible
of a sleeping stag beetle.

(This is a poem about how dragons confuse the creation
of branch shadow patterns with *being* those patterns)

He is gathering the words that pass between
the shadow and the art of the shadow; stone-hidden,
whereabouts unknown.

Facing Night

after Du Fu

Mars appears first. Red, close.
It feeds off the sun's last light.

Prophet of one hundred more
years of war? A breeze moves

through the pears, through
dry hollyhock leaves—lizard-

claws across ancient skin. We
close our eyes. The world is

an abandoned library: creaks,
flapping pages. There are doors

that never fully open, never fully
close. We no longer have names,

faces, and so we move inside,
silent, stars appearing, one by one,

inside our bodies. Tonight, we
can see through our own death.

This Shape

1

An arroyo carved by long-gone water
lures me in. Inside: cracked mud, now
sand, hare shit, prints of horned lizard, deer.
There's a driftwood pile where wind
has gathered branches: snake-chaos, whips,
Chinese calligraphy disassembled, left here
to create a new script . . . or make fire.

2

All the piñon branch-tips that surround
the arroyo are rust-brown: everything is
dying. A missile fired: one part of the
world cheers, one part mourns. Flames
rip across roofs, smoke fills the canyon.
A tunnel of flame spins, creates the wind
that begins the next world.

3

I could have been a rock, a cabbage moth,
a piñon or a dog. Maybe moss or a water-skate.
But I am this shape: small, so small, staring
at the dying piñon. I feel my heart, the ribcage
that surrounds it, the bones in my hands, then
send love out to everyone I know. I have
no idea how to do this. I do it anyway.

Spiral: Self, Community, World, Cosmos

1

Juniper-fall on a ridge:
split-trunk and bleached
branches, blue-splayed
into a spiral.

I walk
around and around
the spiral, looking
for a way in . . .

2

Red light. A woman sells
newspapers on the median.
She's got a routine: razor-sharp
jokes about the president,
his henchmen; playing the fool
to talk about fools. Horrors,
horrors, and I laugh through
the open car window.
She laughs with me. This is
about power, power structures
(literally and in all senses . . .).
The light turns green.

3

Tiangong 1 burns through
the atmosphere: shadows

sail through an orangutan's eyes
in Sumatra, across
Teotihuacan pyramids, over
traffic in Dehli, shoot
through a lone figure
atop Pernal, fall into
a shark's mouth, circling
an island of plastic. In-
visible hands link
indivisible desires
across continents,
an undercurrent beneath
the ceaseless sting
of streetlight, white noise
of office lights
on all night.

4

The radial arm
of a galaxy curves
as it spins, blue-
splayed star-gas
and dust, swinging
across an empty mind.

Something
moves around and around
the spiral, creating
a way in . . .

Lunar New Year

No One

1

The Qi scholar stands in his doorway,
holds a cup of tea with both hands,
breathes in shreds of gray cloud, strips
of blue beyond, scent of rain,
maybe snow, gray wings on a slash pile,
a few desolate drops on flagstone,
a man wiring together a coyote fence,
hired on the cheap, another refugee,
journey worn in the way he lights a cigarette,
the way he stares into the canyon . . .

He has been no one most of his life.

2

The Qi scholar stands in his doorway,
opens his hands. His tea cup is gone,
was never there. The moon, the moon,
one of a thousand identical sisters,
appears, balances on the eastern ridge.
He lets it rest on the end of a finger,
then uses it as a coin to cover both eyes,
practicing blindness, practicing
death.

When did he finally let go
of being someone else's no one
         and choose to be his own?

3

The Qi scholar stands in his doorway,
sticks out his tongue to catch an almost
illusory desert raindrop. Did one land
in his mouth or not? Rain, rain, from
such thin clouds. Patterns, patterns . . .
the way everything is shaped and shapes,
is a map, torn, glowing blue, a song
of unfathomable loss, illuminating
a path to itself. He laughs.

Becoming No One is not a choice.

4

The Qi scholar stands in his doorway.
He has been standing there
for one thousand years. He was
standing there before the doorway
was built. He will be there
after it is gone. He marvels
how trees make mischief at night,
exchange places in the dark, how
a lone snowflake escapes
from a star named Capella, sails
through his forehead, how Capella
is really a system of four stars
in two binary pairs . . .

No One looks at the moon.

Notes

Page 12:
Mozote refers to the village of El Mozote in El
Salvador, site of the El Mozote massacre during the
civil war in December 1981. Close to 1,000 civilians
were killed by the Salvadoran Army unit known as
the Atlacatl Battalion, funded and trained by the
United States through the School of the Americas.

The village of Tokhar is in Syria and is the site of the
Tokhar massacre that occurred in July 2016, carried
out by the United States Air Force. Death toll reports
range from 56 to 212 civilians being killed.

Sangrin is a town in Afghanistan that was bombed by
US forces in 2010 and 2017. The first airstrike, in 2010,
killed 39 civilians, all women and children. After the
second airstrike, in 2017, the United Nations mission
in Afghanistan stated that the strikes had "killed at
least 18 civilians, nearly all women and children."

Page 14:
"No One's at the Cash Register" imitates the style of
Han Shan's poems. Han Shan was a hermit reported
to have lived in the mountains near the Kuo-ch'ing
Temple in southeast China. He sometimes worked
in the temple kitchen and wrote his poems on rocks,
trees, and the walls of farmers' homes. Ever irreverent,
he constantly poked fun at institutional spirituality
and traditional cultural conventions. He took his
poet-name from the place where he lived—Han
Shan translates as Cold Mountain. His poems were

collected after his disappearance. He is reported to have gone into a cave at Cold Cliff after being hassled too many times by temple officials; the cave closed shut, and Han Shan disappeared forever. Han Shan's collection is known as *The Cold Mountain Poems* or *Poems from Cold Mountain*. I like many translations (Snyder, Watson, Red Pine, etc.), but my favorites are the playful, exuberant ones by J. P. Seaton, published by Shambhala Publications.

Page 29:
lemniscate: Any of several figure-eight or ∞-shaped curves. It is used as a symbol for infinity.

Page 60:
haidomyrmex: An extinct genus of ants, known from fossils found in Asia and dating to the late Cretaceous Period.

Page 82:
"Li Bai dove into the moon . . . " Li Po, as Li Bai is still most commonly known in the US, is reported to have died trying to embrace the moon. The apocryphal story says that while drunk he dove off the deck of his riverboat into the moon's reflection and drowned.

About the Author

CHRISTIEN GHOLSON is the author of several books of poetry, including *On the Side of the Crow* (Hanging Loose Press) and *All the Beautiful Dead* (Bitter Oleander Press); along with a novel: *A Fish Trapped Inside the Wind* (Parthian Books). His chapbooks include *The No One Poems* (Thirty West Publishing) and *The Sixth Sense* (Modest Proposal Chapbook series). Several of his chapbooks can be found online, including *Tidal Flats* (Mudlark) and *How the World was Made* (2River View). He has been many shapes before attaining congenial form: factory worker, cashier, crow feather resting on snow, bookseller, editor, crab leg tangled in seaweed, teacher, farmhand, ochre handprint on a cave wall, union organizer and wanderer. He attended Naropa University; University of California, Davis; and Southwestern College in Santa Fe, New Mexico. His work has appeared in *Ecotone, Permafrost, Another Chicago Magazine, Banyan Review, The Shore, Hotel Amerika, Alaska Quarterly Review, Tiger Moth Review*, and *The Sun*, among many other literary journals. He spent many years living in northcentral New Mexico where the poems in *Absence ♦ Presence* were written. He now works as a somatic-oriented therapist in Oregon.

—christiengholson.blogspot.com

SHANTI ARTS

NATURE ▪ ART ▪ SPIRIT

Please visit us online
to browse our entire book catalog,
including poetry collections and fiction,
books on travel, nature, healing, art,
photography, and more.

Also take a look at our highly regarded art
and literary journal, *Still Point Arts Quarterly*,
which may be downloaded for free.

www.shantiarts.com